Always Reforming

Reflections on the 500th Anniversary of the Reformation

Steven P. Mueller, editor

Contributors

Clinton J. Armstrong, Scott A. Ashmon,
Russell P. Dawn, Katherine Dubke,
Paul M. C. Elliott, Michael A. Eschelbach,
David W. Loy, Michael P. Middendorf,
Steven P. Mueller, David L. Rueter

ISBN: 197588714X
ISBN-13: 978-1975887148

Always Reforming

CONTENTS

ACKNOWLEDGMENTS

The writings in this volume were produced for the 500th anniversary of the Reformation by Concordia University Irvine. We are thankful for all who supported this work, especially Quinton Anderson, Ann Ashmon, Carrie Donohoe, Rick Hardy, Jeff Held, Bil Hood, Kurt Krueger, Amy Lucker, Sarah Pak, and all of the contributing authors. We are blessed to serve with them.

ABOUT THE COVER

"We Witness Now" is a mural created by Gerald F. Brommer in 1961. It was commissioned for Los Angeles Lutheran High School. It now is part of Concordia University Irvine's art collection.

ALWAYS REFORMING

Five hundred years ago, an Augustinian monk and professor objected to abuses in the Medieval Church. He probably didn't know where his 95 points for debate would lead. Rather, seeing problems in his church, he sought to reform it from the inside. Sadly, his call to return to the teachings of Scripture—to the proclamation of salvation by grace, through faith in Christ and not by human works—was not always well received. But since the teaching came from Scripture, it endured.

The Reformation began on that day and quickly spread, affecting all Christian churches. Its effects continue today. The changes that it launched in the church and in broader society were wide reaching. It is truly a historic event.

Christians whose churches arose out of the Reformation may celebrate these events, even as they should mourn divisions in the church. However, in remembering these important things, let us not lose sight of an important truth: the church is always reforming.

The church is always reforming, not because God changes or the truth changes. No, it is always reforming because the church is made up of human beings. Every one of them sinful. Every one of them tempted to ignore the word of God or to substitute his or her own ideas for God's truth. It is easy for Christians, and for churches, to become confused and to drift from God's Word and will.

When that happens to churches, God calls them to return. "Come back to me," he says. "Leave these flawed ideas of yours and come back to my truth." That happened in the Reformation, but it keeps happening repeatedly. "Let me bring you back," God says. He will! He is always reforming his church.

We see the same thing in individual lives. If we are honest, it is easier to see in our own lives than anywhere else. Individual Christians need reformation. Daily we sin and seek our own way. Still, God is faithful. In love, He calls us back to himself. "Repent. Turn around. Come to me. Let me re-form you. Let me shape you once more into what you were always meant to be: my child!"

In this, the 500th anniversary year of the Reformation, God calls all people to himself, just as he does every day. "My grace is for you. Come and let me bless you."

Thank God that he re-forms us each day.

IT STARTED ON ALL SAINTS' DAY

Who are these, clothed in white robes, and from where have they come?" … These are the ones coming out of the great tribulation. They have washed their robes and made them white in the blood of the Lamb.

–Revelation 7:9–10, 13–14

Now therefore, if you will indeed obey my voice and keep my covenant, you shall be my treasured possession among all peoples, for all the earth is mine; and you shall be to me a kingdom of priests and a holy nation.

–Exodus 19:5–6

You are a chosen race, a royal priesthood, a holy nation, a people for his own possession, that you may proclaim the excellencies of him who called you out of darkness into his marvelous light. Once you were not a people, but now you are God's people; once you had not received mercy, but now you have received mercy.

–1 Peter 2:9–10

Pilgrims wend to Wittenberg.

Maybe this All Saints' Day will count for something. Perhaps these relics: a bone, a scrap of wood or a shred of cloth once worn by the holy ones will help. Maybe some of their sanctity will rub off on sinners, on me.

Seeking something to make them right with God.

Remembering the faithful.

Begging mercy for the departed with more checkered lives.

Anxious for themselves, they come.

But few are recognized this day. Only the rare few are holy here below. Maybe them. Not me. Sainthood is beyond my reach.

Pilgrims come forgetting the words spoken to Israel: "You shall be to me a kingdom of priests and a holy nation" (Exodus 19:6).

But even the holy nation forgot that God made them holy and, making it their work, they failed. They forgot that they were redeemed to be a kingdom of priests.

We forget. God remembers, proclaiming again in the new covenant:

> Once you were not a people, but now you are God's people; once you had not received mercy, but now you have received mercy. –1 Peter 2:9-10

That truth is proclaimed again each day. You—the Baptized, redeemed by Christ alone, saved by grace alone—you are holy. Saints. Priests of our God.

People of God. Chosen, belonging to him, called into light. You are his royal priests offering yourselves as living sacrifices of praise to the One who sacrificed his flesh for you.

Pilgrims to Wittenberg, seeking saints, find theses instead. Theses that turn pilgrims away from themselves. Theses that turn them, not toward saints, but to Christ who declares sinners to be holy saints.

Pilgrims, remember the faithful departed: those redeemed by Christ. And rejoice that in Jesus, we are ALL Saints.

THE STORY OF THE REFORMATION

Late in 1517, Martin Luther was a little-known monk and professor at a new university in Wittenberg, Germany, a minor town on the outskirts of the Holy Roman Empire. Although he had previously taught against unscriptural doctrines, he was virtually invisible to the powers in Rome.

Invisible, that is, until he stepped into the indulgence controversy. The papal court was participating in an elaborate financial scheme whereby the sale of indulgences—papal certificates to forgive sins—would help finance the rebuilding of St. Peter's Basilica in Rome. When Luther heard of these sales in a neighboring area, he wrote 95 theses for academic disputation, condemning the sale of indulgences. When, on October 31st of that year, he nailed the theses to the door of Wittenberg's Castle Church, they were soon copied and widely dispersed. Suddenly Luther was quite visible, directly in the cross-hairs of the papal court.

Many prominent voices in Luther's time were critical of the corrupt papacy, but Luther's message was different. He called not only for moral change, but for theological reform. The sale of indulgences was merely a symptom of departures from Scriptural teachings such as justification by grace alone, through faith alone, for the sake of Christ alone. Luther was soon excommunicated, and his teachings banned.

He was not easily silenced, however. He preached, taught, and wrote prolifically, all the while longing for Mother Church to return in unity to her apostolic roots. There appeared to be an opportunity in 1530, when Emperor Charles V called for a meeting of imperial leaders at Augsburg. The goal was to heal the religious differences that plagued the Empire from within, while the Turks were a threat from without. The Lutherans presented a sound and winsome case in the Augsburg Confession, but the papal faction was hardened against their teachings. Religion would remain a dividing factor in the Empire, and Luther's reform would remain a reformation, an institutional division that marks the church even today.

The church is called to proclaim biblical truth, particularly the saving Gospel of Christ crucified and resurrected. This cannot be compromised. At the same time, the faithful join in Jesus' prayer for the unity of the church—a unity in the truth. Confident in the Gospel, we pray and work for the unity of the church, which is redeemed by Christ and always reforming.

THE CONSERVING REFORMATION

When Martin Luther posted his 95 theses for debate, he was addressing challenges in his church, seeking discussion and correction. He certainly did not intend to give rise to a separate branch of the Christian church—much less one that would come to be called by his name. Nevertheless, when his call to reform was rejected, this is exactly what occurred.

While this was a notable development, it was not as radical as some people think. This was not a revolution but a restoration or reformation. Luther and his colleagues did not start a new church. They reformed the church. They did not throw everything out and start over again. That would not have been an appropriate response. For while reformation was certainly needed, there were many good and commendable things in the church. Things worth preserving and even celebrating.

So while some later branches of Christianity made more radical cuts and changes, Luther's principle was to retain anything that was not contrary to the word of God.

Therefore, the Lutheran Confessions say things like:

> ...private absolution should be retained and not abolished
>
> –Augsburg Confession XI:1

> [We retain] many ceremonies and traditions such as the order of the Mass and other singing, festivals and the like, which serve to preserve order in the church
>
> –Augsburg Confession XXVI:40

> [We desire to] retain the order of the church and the various ranks of the church—even though they were established by human authority
>
> –Apology to the Augsburg Confession XIV:24

In contrast, things that the reformers thought were in conflict with biblical teaching had to be changed. For as good as it is to preserve many things, above all,

> ...it is necessary to retain in the church the pure teaching concerning the righteousness of faith.
>
> –Apology to the Augsburg Confession IV: iii, 237

This approach is sometimes called the conservative reformation, but perhaps a more helpful way to understand it would be to call it a conserving reformation. It strives to retain the best practices of the historic church, integrating them in a contemporary context. It is always to be guided by the teachings of Scripture and the centrality of the Gospel of Jesus Christ.

The church today—always reforming—can learn from this approach. The best practices of our Christian forebears can be very helpful in our context. And all of our practice is to be guided by Scripture and focused on the Gospel.

SOLA SCRIPTURA

From childhood you have been acquainted with the sacred writings, which are able to make you wise for salvation through faith in Christ Jesus. All Scripture is breathed out by God and profitable for teaching, for reproof, for correction, and for training in righteousness, that the man of God may be complete, equipped for every good work.

–2 Timothy 3:15–17

Word alone, breathed by the Spirit,
Word revealing Christ our Lord,
Living, active voice of Jesus,
Sharper than a two-edged sword.
Word to teach and to admonish,
Word to comfort and to heal.
God's own Word endures forever
All his counsel to reveal.

SOLA SCRIPTURA: WORD ALONE

One of the great and lasting themes of the Reformation was a return to Holy Scripture. In an era when Bibles were not available in the language of the people, and knowledge of the contents of Holy Scripture was woefully lacking, this was desperately needed. It seems so obvious to Christians today, but at the time, this return to the original, inspired sources was a radical change.

Sola Scriptura—Scripture Alone—affirms the primacy of the Bible. The source of Christian teaching must be the word of God, and Christian life and teaching must be shaped and evaluated by that word. It all comes from God. We may learn from tradition and learned authority. We reflect on our own experiences and use the reason that God gave us to think and to contemplate different ideas. But Reformation theology recognizes that all of these things are impacted by sin and so are imperfect. Nevertheless, one source is perfect. "All Scripture is breathed out by God and profitable for teaching, for reproof, for correction, and for training in righteousness" (2 Timothy 3:16). Jesus himself teaches us that God's Word is truth (John 17:17).

The Reformation era insight is just as important for Christians today. God's word is a gift to us. It informs and guides our teaching and lives.

THE BIBLE FOR EVERYONE

"What will happen if anyone can read the Bible?" This was one of the objections hurled against Martin Luther by the religious authorities of his day. Luther replied, "I suppose more people will become Christians." Luther's translation of the Scriptures into German was one of his greatest accomplishments.

The determination of Martin Luther (and others like Tyndale and Wycliffe) to translate the Bible into the language of the people was inspired by the very text they wanted to translate. The Lord Jesus commanded us to make disciples of all nations, in part by immersing them in his word (Matthew 28:18–20) and to be ambassadors for Christ, extending to all the good news of our reconciliation to God through Jesus. How are we to do that unless the people hear (Romans 10:13–17)?

The Bible itself advocates translation and faithful explanation. Ezra read the word to the people and explained it to them. The apostles John and Paul included translations and explanations of terms in their writing. The entire Old Testament was translated into Greek more than two centuries before the birth of Jesus and the New Testament often quotes this translation (called the Septuagint).

The Bible also conveys great confidence about God, his word, and his Spirit's ability to see to it that the one who "remains in his word" does, in fact, come to know the truth that makes one a disciple in truth and makes one free (John 8:31-32). Peter explained that the Bible is not of one's own private interpretation (2 Peter 1:20). Paul urged that the Bible must be understood according to the analogy of faith (Romans 12:6).

The corruption that abides in our human nature will always seek to corrupt any truth, including the word of God. Only the word of God has the power to drown this old Adam, to bury it with Christ by baptism into death and to regenerate and bring forth each day a new man who will live before God in righteousness and purity forever. Hearing and reading God's Word, Christians are always reforming.

LAW & GOSPEL

Healing is a gift of God—a universal human experience that bears witness to God's will that we should live. While bodily systems often bring about healing without intervention, some ailments require surgery. The surgeon's knife does not do the healing, but provides better circumstances for healing to take place. It is precisely for this reason that the surgeon cuts.

Martin Luther recognized that the word of God brings a different kind of healing through the Law and Gospel. "Law" describes what God requires. It demands perfection: a standard we cannot meet. "Gospel" describes what God provides so that we may live. The Law is like the surgeon's knife, cutting the sin that corrupts our lives and brings death. The Gospel is healing. It is the most profound healing since it is eternal and heals in every way.

Without the Law, we do not see that we are spiritually sick, and so will not receive the healing that is offered. We see this in the Gospel of Mark as a lawyer came to Jesus in order to justify himself, claiming that he had kept the Law. But since he only looked to himself and not to God, he was unable to fix his spiritual problem. He went away under the condemnation of the Law (Mark 10:17–22). In contrast, many came to Jesus with nothing but a plea of helplessness and need; Jesus provided what they needed and more.

Giving the grace of God (Gospel) to a person who claims to keep the Law perfectly is ineffective because the self-righteous person sees no need for grace and may even think it is insulting. They don't see that they are sick. But when God's grace is given to a person burdened and afraid under the condemnation of the Law, they find restoration, healing, and new life in Christ.

God's purpose is always healing. He shows us our sin so that we are ready to receive the perfect healing that comes when the work of Jesus is applied to us.

The church—and Christians—are always reforming as they hear the Law and are restored by the Gospel.

LUTHER & BIBLICAL INTERPRETATION

The most famous event of 1517 is Luther's posting of his 95 Theses. However, in the same year Luther reached a milestone that may be even more significant: he finally abandoned the medieval method of interpreting the Bible.

For centuries, the dominant way of interpreting the Scriptures assigned four separate meanings to each thing.

For example, when the Bible speaks about Jerusalem, medieval theologians said that it was talking about

1) The city in Israel (literal),
2) The church (allegorical),
3) The soul (moral), and
4) Heaven (eschatological).

Luther identified the shortcomings of this approach, which was too often dependent upon guesswork and the whims of the interpreter. He wrote,

> It was very difficult for me to break away from my habitual zeal for allegory. And yet I was aware that allegories were empty speculations and the froth, as it were, of the Holy Scriptures. It is the historical sense alone which supplies the true and sound doctrine (*Luther's Works* I:283).

Luther identified that the Scriptures had one sense, the literal or natural sense. This did not mean that he was a complete literalist. For example, he stated that figures of speech are meant to be taken figuratively. However, when the Scriptures speak plainly, they should be taken literally according to the normal use of language. The implication of this approach is that the Bible is clear in its meaning and can be understood by ordinary people.

The most important principle of interpretation that Martin Luther used was "Scripture interprets Scripture." The tools for properly interpreting the Bible are contained in the Bible itself. Thus, he delved into the New Testament to see how Jesus and the apostles had interpreted Scripture. There he found a valuable tool. He discovered that many Old Testament people and institutions were to be understood as types or patterns that foreshadowed and proclaimed the Christ, who would surpass them and fulfill them. Thus, in his *Preface to the Psalter*, Luther wrote, "The true, the only sense of the Psalms is the Christ-sense."

For Luther, every part of the Bible proclaimed Christ, not apart from the literal sense, but in a way that was communicated by the literal sense. Luther "desired to know nothing but Christ crucified" (1 Corinthians 2:2), and we continue in that legacy when we speak the Christ-filled message of Scripture.

GOD HASN'T LIED TO ME YET

A simple person armed with Scripture is
greater than the mightiest pope without it.

How do you know what you know?
You can reach deep inside and promote self-inspection,
You can do a great service through thought and reflection,
Grave meditation and deep introspection –

But how do you know what you know?

You can learn things from teachers, from parents, from classes.
From priests, from the news, gurus peering through glasses.
You can learn a great deal from this world's wise sophomores—

But how do you know what you know?

Praise science, arts, and observations;
Laud all our dreamers' contemplations—
God yet speaks—a Revelation.

And God hasn't lied to me yet.

In the beginning was the Word. And the Word was with God. And the Word was God.

The Word became flesh and dwelt among us.

The Word—the very accessible Word, the divine Word, the human Word, the Word you can understand because the Word became like you.

The Word who shows you who he is in words. Words in Hebrew, words in Greek,

Words in Spanish, words in German, Chinese, French and Kiswahili. Words that call him Lord and Savior.

The Word who shows you who you are in words. Words that call you sinner, saint. Breathed out by God. To correct you. Rebuke you. Teach you. Train you to righteousness—to equip you for the good works he has already in mind, that you should walk in them.

The Word who reveals himself in words, the Christ, the center of the scripture, a very sure defense. "These are the words which I spoke to you while I was yet with you, that all things must be fulfilled which were written in the Law of Moses and in the Prophets and in the Psalms concerning ME!"

Words in ink, words on paper, the commonest things around. The Word who is our prophet, priest, and king: this prophet's pen, mightier than any sword. The Word they still shall let remain, nor any thanks have for it, whether devils, angels, councils, popes, or anything else in all creation:

How do you know what you know?

Let God be true and every man a liar. 'Cause God hasn't lied to me yet.

SOLA GRATIA

For by grace you have been saved through faith. And this is not your own doing; it is the gift of God, not a result of works, so that no one may boast. For we are his workmanship, created in Christ Jesus for good works, which God prepared beforehand, that we should walk in them.

–Ephesians 2:8–10

Grace alone, and not our working,
Brings salvation unto all.
Grace alone! Your gifts you give us
As we hear your gentle call.
Unimagined love, exchanging
All our sin for righteousness.
Grace on grace through Christ receiving,
Clothed in his own holiness.

SOLA GRATIA: GRACE ALONE

"How can I be saved?" we ask, or "How can I be right with God?" Left to our own devices, the human answer is remarkably consistent: be good. Work hard to do good things and avoid bad things, and maybe it will all turn out right. This seems to make sense—until we try putting it into practice. How much is enough? How can I ever be sure that I will be OK?

The Reformation began with the recognition that we are not able to overcome our own sin. No work or effort we do can ever be sufficient. Our sin is too great and our works too poor. Left to ourselves, we rightly despair. This is where Martin Luther found himself. But then he read, "In [the Gospel] the righteousness of God is revealed from faith to faith, as it is written, 'The righteous shall live by faith'" (Romans 1:17). Here is God's answer: Grace.

Grace is God's undeserved favor, love, and mercy towards humanity because of the work of Christ. It is a gift. God freely gives us what we could never deserve.

Nothing we can ever do would be enough. But Christ is. God does it all for us.

> By grace you have been saved through faith. And this is not your own doing; it is the gift of God, not a result of works, so that no one may boast.
>
> –Ephesians 2:8

Salvation is a free gift from God. We are saved by grace alone.

GRACE ALONE: THE LORD SPEAKS

I don't see you the way that she sees you. Different lenses.

I don't see you the way he sees you. I have a different perspective.

I don't see you the way that they see you. I look at different things.

I don't even see you the way that YOU see you.

Because when you look at yourself, you preen, you strut. You make things up with makeup. You dress for success, you imagine your image is in—and you'd better if you want to chase the next dollar, make the next cut, climb the next step in your career.

When you look at yourself, you test, you examine, you poke and you prod, and you wonder how long you can put off seeing the physician. The dentist. The dietician, the urologist, the oncologist.

When you look at yourself, you see your history. The wrinkles. The lines. The scars. The age, and with it the regrets, staring back at you in a mirror that remembers, eyes catching your own and peering into you, glancing at the past, recollections of deeds gone wrong, goods avoided, sparks that fanned shames into full, fiery flames.

But I see through your pride. I see through your pain. I see through the shame. I've never avoided looking at you. I see you all the time. I just see something different.

Not just "the real you," as if there's a special little sunbeam deep inside you. No. Stop fooling yourself.

Not just "the potential inside you," either, as if there's something good waiting just around the corner. Stop putting your faith in fake news and fairy tales.

And not just the résumé, the vita, the rap sheet, as if the sum of you is all the crimes you've ever done.

No, I see something different. Different lenses. Different perspective. I look at different things.

Because the one I love most is Jesus. The one I love most is my Son. The one I love most is the apple of my eye.

When I look at what he did. What he suffered, the eye in the storm. How he died. How he rose. How he took the world in his hands and handed it back to me. When I look at Jesus, that's as far as my eye can see.

It's changed everything for me, the way I see things. Beauty is in my eye now, the beauty of Jesus. Beauty is in the eye of the beholder, and now your ugliness is beautiful.

His humility is in my eye now, and now your pride is his meekness and lowliness.

His death is in my eye now, and now all your striving, all your scrambling for survival, in all of it I see only his death.

And his life, his new life, his resurrected, glorious life, that's what's in my eye now, and now your pain, your weakness, your handicap, your sickness, now your darkness and death, in all of it I see only life. Life in him, life in you, life for all, life forever.

My glasses aren't blind to who you really are.

My glasses aren't rose-colored optimism, rooting for you to do your best.

My glasses are Christ-tinted, Jesus-shaded, taking you, the real you, the you of your past, present, and always, the you at your worst, seeing you in your sinfulness, perceiving you in your pride and your pain, glancing at your depravity, glimpsing at your death. But in my grace—alone in my grace—in my grace alone, I see not your ego, your self, your infection, your fall, your failings and felonies and faults.

In my grace, alone in my grace—in my grace alone, I see Jesus. Now that's a sight for sore eyes.

RESPONDING TO GRACE

Captured by hidden cameras, a young man gave $100 to a stunned homeless person begging by a freeway onramp. And then, secretly, skeptically, he watched to see how it would be spent. First to a liquor store, then to a park. But not to get drunk. No—to give food purchased at the liquor store to other homeless people.

Real or hoax? Either way, this viral video illustrates a response. In our better moments, unexpected blessings are sometimes paid forward.

Sure self-centered, broken people may hoard blessings, exploit generosity, or turn a blind eye to others' needs. But sometimes, a surprising blessing gets shared.

How can it be that the poor are generous? That the hungry share food? That needs are met when those who have plenty of needs themselves share with others?

Because those who have nothing and receive everything know what it means.

Grace asks nothing of us. God looks upon us unworthy, unloving, undeserving creatures and—despite what we are—chooses to be himself. Gracious!

While we were sinners. Enemies of God. Hostile to his love. Turned in on ourselves. Helpless. Hopeless. Dead. Even then—especially then—we see who God is. Gracious!

Grace asks nothing of us, but the new life that it creates springs forth. With hunger satisfied, how can we not share food with others who still hunger? When we are loved, love can overflow. Forgiveness received from God can, by faith, be shared with others.

And in responding, we find that God's grace is never exhausted. We receive "grace upon grace." He invites us to receive, and then graces us again by letting us know joy in sharing his mercy and grace.

SOLA FIDE

Faith is "a living, busy, active, mighty thing."
–Martin Luther

Faith alone, gift of the Spirit,
Can God's gracious gift receive.
Not by human works or effort,
God is calling to believe.
Faith is living, busy, active,
Ever seeking ways to care,
In the least, the lost, the needy,
Seeking Jesus everywhere.

SOLA FIDE: FAITH ALONE

> By grace you have been saved through faith. And this is not your own doing; it is the gift of God, not a result of works, so that no one may boast.
>
> –Ephesians 2:8-9

We are saved by God's grace alone. But how do we receive that grace?

Somehow, we always seem to try to put ourselves back in control of God's work. "I've got to do something, don't I?"

Yet even here, we see the grace of God. He only asks that we receive his gift by faith. "Believe," he says. "Let me give you this free gift.

Even faith itself is a gift of God, created by the Holy Spirit. "No one can say 'Jesus is Lord' except in the Holy Spirit" (1 Corinthians 12:3). We were dead in our trespasses and sins, but God has made us alive in Christ. God provides all that is needed when he makes us his children. He creates this new life in us.

This faith clings to Jesus alone as Savior. Luther said that faith is a living, daring confidence in God's grace. It trusts God, and sees that all good things come from him.

Though faith in Christ is a gift of God, that does not mean that the Christian never responds. Once faith is kindled, it moves into action. It does not try to earn God's favor. Rather, it joyfully and freely responds to the gifts it has received. So Luther also said that "faith is a living, busy, active, mighty thing." It seeks opportunities to bless others as we have been blessed.

We are not saved by our works, but by faith alone. And that is how Christians are called to live: confidently trusting God, and boldly serving our neighbor.

LIVING THE REFORMATION FAITH

Living out the Reformation faith is simple. It isn't easy, but it is not complicated. Before I came to this faith, I found myself frequently tied into knots over the question of whether I was living out God's plan for my life. Had God planned for me to be in my chosen profession, or had I strayed from his will? Did he want me involved in this ministry or that one? I even wondered whether it was his will that I marry my beloved fiancé! Continually I strained to see signs that my path was God's chosen one for me. Forget about the peace that passes understanding, I didn't even have ordinary peace.

I became Lutheran 11 years ago, and it didn't take long for me to find new peace—or rather, for peace to find me. To live the Reformation faith is to live at the foot of the cross of Christ. That's it. That always was and always will be God's plan for my life, and for the lives of all Christians. There is no secret path or hidden sign we must discern on threat of being outside of God's will. At the foot of the cross we love God and give him thanks and praise. We pray to him there. We receive all that is needful for salvation there. As Christ died there in service to us and for our benefit, so we die to ourselves in service to our neighbors and for their benefit. What sort of service? Whatever our neighbors need that we can provide. In any career, whether as spouse or as friend, serving those who know they need it, or those who do not realize that they need to be served—opportunities to serve come to us as gift. We are blessed in serving. No strings attached. No fine print. And when we serve, our service comes to our neighbors as gift.

Jesus promised us peace when we come to him. To live in the faith of the Reformation is to dwell at the foot of the cross, loving God and serving neighbor, and receiving Christ's peace.

PRODUCING FRUIT

Faith or works? Reformation era debates about the distinction and place of faith and works continue today. The debate rears its head as some insist that Christianity must produce "results." We see it in Bible studies and Sunday school lessons that confuse the Gospel of Jesus Christ with moral instruction. At its worst, some Christians think that their salvation is based on their being a "good person."

The confusion heads down a different path when Christians seem to ignore the will of God and see the Gospel as an excuse to sin.

In these opposite errors, we see that there is truly nothing new under the sun!

Luther struggled with the book of James because he saw the potential to misread the apostle's admonition.

> So also faith by itself, if it does not have works, is dead.
>
> –James 2:17

He did not see how that reconciled with Paul's words:

> For we hold that one is justified by faith apart from works of the law.
>
> –Romans 3:28

However when these passages are read in the context of Christ's teachings and the rest of Scripture, we find something else. Good works are not the cause of our salvation. They are the fruit of faith. They are Christ's work through us, not our work through Christ. Jesus says:

> I am the vine; you are the branches. Whoever abides in me and I in him, he it is that bears much fruit, for apart from me you can do nothing.
>
> –John 15: 5

As a branch, I am not able to produce fruit by my own efforts. Rather, through my abiding in the vine, fruit is produced by Christ in my life.

This is so incredibly freeing! I do not need to struggle to appease God or to pay him back, rather as Luther put it:

> God does not need your good works, but your neighbor does.

I don't need to purchase anything or spend my life wondering if I have done enough. Christ has done enough! Now, in faith, I simply abide in Christ, in Word and Sacrament, and with the community of the church. My life will serve anyone God places in my life. God works through us to bear fruit.

FAITH ALONE

We hold that one is justified by faith apart from works of the law.

–Romans 3:28

Without faith it is impossible to please him

–Hebrews 11:6

By grace you have been saved through faith. And this is not your own doing; it is the gift of God

–Ephesians 2:8

"Catch me, Daddy!" With gleeful, trusting boldness, children leap into the waiting arms of their parents, confident that they are safe. They will be caught.

Unless their trust has been broken, they know that Mom and Dad will not let them fall. Even to their peril, at times, they trust their imperfect parents.

Trust is reinforced from infancy—even the womb. A fussing newborn knows her mother's voice in a crowd. Toddlers are certain their parents can do whatever they say. Parents are their own superheroes. No one is like *their* mommy or daddy.

And then we learn. Some leaps are foolhardy. Parents cannot always catch us. Failures undermine trust and sow uncertainty.

And growing independence asserts itself. "No! I do it! Don't help. I don't need you." Curved in on ourselves, we do not want to be reliant, dependent, beholden to anyone. We do not want to receive. We want to be in control.

We call it maturing. It is necessary for human development, even if painful. Emerging independence is important, but it can grieve a parent.

Yet no matter how independent they are, they are always my children.

With gleeful abandon, the child of God cries out: "Catch me!" and knows that this Father will not fail.

Luther said, "Faith is a daring confidence in God's grace, so sure and certain that a man could stake his life on it a thousand times."

God is that trustworthy.

The Christian Faith has content. Ideas matter. Truth matters. But faith is no mere idea. It is not a philosophical construct or system.

Faith trusts. Faith receives. Faith knows that God is faithful even when minds struggle to comprehend.

Children lead the way. Our Lord himself blessed children (Mark 10:16). The kingdom of God belongs to such as these (Luke 18:16) "Whoever does not receive the kingdom of God like a child shall not enter it" (Luke 18:17).

Could it be that our false maturity, our stubborn, self-centered, inwardly focused independence pushes God away? Do we shout: "No, I do it!" or "I don't need you!"?

No matter how foolishly independent we are, he is our Father, and we are his children. He calls us to faith in Christ again. To trust.

Faith is bold because it is specific. It is faith in Christ. Faith trusts and receives, knowing that needs are provided from his gracious abundance.

Even the faith that receives God's blessings is itself a gift. A gift that enlivens. A gift, created by the Spirit, that receives the free gifts of God. Faith—faith alone—is the only things that receives.

By grace you have been saved, through faith, and this not of yourselves, it is a gift of God.

It is all a gift from our loving Father. The one who always holds us in his watchful care. The God who provides. The God of grace and mercy who saves.

Joyful faith, knowing the voice of our perfect, loving Father, boldly cries out: "Catch me, Father!"

And God stretches his strong arms wide—on a cross—to catch the whole world.

SOLUS CHRISTUS

"There is salvation in no one else, for there is no other name under heaven given among men by which we must be saved.

–Acts 4:12

Christ alone the world's redeemer,
Christ, God's own begotten Son,
Christ, the sacrifice for sinners,
By his death salvation won.
Christ alone our mediator,
Christ alone our great high priest,
In his righteousness, he clothes us.
Christ alone is our true peace.

JUSTIFIED!

Martin Luther was an Augustinian monk, schooled in the thought of the great Christian teacher, St. Augustine of Hippo. However, Augustine's description of justification negatively affected what Luther initially believed about justification and righteousness before God.

The two parts of the word "justification" illustrate the point. The latter part comes from the Latin *facio* from which we get the English word "factory." It is a place where you "make" or "do" things. Thus, the Latin term literally means "make just." Augustine's view, called "sanitive justification," conveys a process by which God works progressively to cleanse or purify believers in order to make them just. Only when God has completed this work can a person stand before him as righteous (Saarnivaara, Luther Discovers the Gospel, CPH, 2005, pp. 6-9).

Luther took God's Law seriously and realized his human nature had not yet been made righteous. Far from it! He wrote,

> I felt that I was a sinner before God with an extremely disturbed conscience. I

> could not believe that [God] was placated by my satisfaction. I did not love, yes, I hated the righteous God who punished sinners.

When Luther uncovered the legal or forensic nature of the Greek words used in the New Testament, the essence of the Gospel was revealed to him. The words stem from the courtroom and convey the declaration of a judge. St. Paul's prominent use teaches that justification or righteousness before God comes from outside of us. It is not based upon who we are or even how righteous we might become; indeed, in this world we will always fall short. Instead, we are what God declares us to be: righteous and holy before him. This is true only because Christ himself is our "righteousness, sanctification and redemption" (1 Corinthians 1:30; cf. 6:11).

What a difference this made in Luther's understanding! He states:

> I began to understand that the righteousness of God is that by which the righteous lives by a gift of God, namely by faith. And this is the meaning: the righteousness of God is revealed by the gospel, namely the passive righteousness with which merciful God justifies us by faith. (*Luther's Works* 34:336-337; citing Romans 1:17).

A hymn eloquently summarizes this by praising God, because: "Thy strong Word bespeaks us righteous" (*Lutheran Service Book* 578:3).

God is always reforming each Christian as, daily, he declares us righteous for Christ's sake.

CHRIST ALONE

Jesus Christ is the same. Yesterday. Today. Forever.

As it was in the beginning.

When God sang creation into being, the lyric of his song was God the Word, making, generating, producing and multiplying.

In the image of God created he man, male and female he created them. The founder and author of a perfect creation was God the Word, second person of the Trinity, the glorious son of God, *ha Dabar*, *ho Logos*, *das Wort*, ¡*la Palabra*! The Word.

Why do you ask my name? It is wonderful! As it was in the beginning:

Wonderful. Counselor. Almighty God. The everlasting Father. The prince of peace.

The prince promised of old, after wreck and spoilage had wreaked ruin on our foremothers and forefathers for their fault and offense, fallen in sin.

The prince promised by prophets proclaiming a savior to come, the God of Abraham, the Fear of Isaac, David's son yet David's Lord.

A great good shepherd to gather his flock.

A king born as angels sang peace on earth to men on whom God's favor rests.

The Word who took on flesh so that all who received him, all who believed on his name, should be called children of God.

The son of Mary, the Son of God, the one who is Immanuel, God with us, the one who is named Jesus because he saves his people from their sins.

The Jesus who is himself our peace, by whose blood you who once were far off have been brought near.

The Jesus who is himself alone our peace, who has made us both one and has broken down in his flesh the dividing wall of hostility.

The Jesus whose flesh was killed, the Jesus whose flesh was raised, the Jesus who in the flesh will come again.

As it was in the beginning, is now.

The flesh of Christ ascended to heaven. The flesh of Christ delivered to you. The body of Christ for you and in you. The body of Christ, his Church, built strong to endure on the rock of his Word, against which the gates of hell will never prevail.

The body of Christ, of which you are his members, you his hands, you his feet, Christ for your neighbor, Christ for the world, Christ alone.

Salvation is found in no one else, for there is no other name under heaven by which we must be saved.

As it was in the beginning, is now, and ever shall be, unto ages of ages.

Jesus Christ, the same yesterday. Today. And forever.

Christ alone.

THE REFORMATION SINGS

When Luther published an evangelical revision of the Latin Mass (*The Order of Mass and Communion*, 1523), he called for poets to write new hymns. A prolific period of Christian hymnody began almost immediately. Some hymns were German translations of earlier texts. Some were adaptations of religious folk songs, and some were newly written. (One of the most enduring myths of the Reformation is that Luther turned drinking songs into hymns. Despite the popularity of this notion, there is no evidence to support it.)

Luther himself wrote 38 hymns, many of which are still in use today. His most famous hymn, "A Mighty Fortress is our God," is a paraphrase of Psalm 46. He wrote both the words and the music.

Luther's first known hymn is less familiar. On July 1, 1523, two Augustinian friars in the Netherlands were burned at the stake when they would not recant the evangelical teachings that they learned from Luther.

Deeply moved by their faithful confession, Luther wrote a ballad so that their story would be remembered. It begins with a common opening line and continues with their story.

> A new song here shall be begun
> The Lord God help our singing!
> Of what our God himself hath done,
> Praise, honor to him bringing,
> At Brussels in the Netherlands
> By two boys, martyrs youthful
> He showed the wonders of his hands,
> Whom he with favor truthful
> So richly hath adorned. (LW 53:214–216)

In twelve stanzas, he goes on to tell the story of their martyrdom.

Luther penned many more hymns. He wrote songs that paraphrased the major parts of the liturgy. Each chief part of the catechism had a corresponding hymn that helped people learn and remember the Ten Commandments, the Apostles' Creed, the Lord's Prayer, and other teachings. And, of course, he wrote hymns that summarize biblical texts.

Like many others before and after him, Luther used music to worship God and to communicate Christian teaching effectively.

This pattern continues today, as many carry out this same work of creating music for the church. The Reformation sings as the church is always reforming.

PRAYER

> A Christian without prayer is just as impossible as a living person without a pulse. The pulse is never motionless; it moves and beats constantly, whether one is asleep or something else keeps one from being aware of it.
>
> –Martin Luther (*Luther's Works*, 24:89)

Martin Luther valued prayer. Once he wrote a short book for his barber, Peter Beskendorf, called "A Simple Way to Pray" (*Luther's Works* 43:193-211). In it, Luther described a pattern of devotions for his friend, noting that it was his own practice. He prayed the Lord's Prayer, considering how each petition addressed his situation that day. Elsewhere, he demonstrated the same idea with prayers based on the Ten Commandments and the Apostles' Creed. In these reflections, he looked to each teaching for instruction, thanksgiving, confession, and petition.

Luther's teachings on prayer include his explanation to the Lord's Prayer in both the Small and Large Catechisms. One can easily see that Luther is teaching how to pray and not just about prayer. The same applied teaching can be seen as he paraphrases the Lord's Prayer into his hymn, "Our Father, Who from Heaven Above" (*Lutheran Service Book* 766).

Luther gave further examples of prayer in the Small Catechism with morning and evening prayers, and prayers for before and after meals.

Luther's faith is seen in his prayers, as is his pastoral love and concern for others. He wanted all Christians to pray gladly and frequently, since

> God tenderly invites us to believe that he is our true Father and that we are his true children, so that with all boldness and confidence we may ask him as dear children ask their dear father.
>
> –Small Catechism:
> The Lord's Prayer

TWO HYMN TEXTS
I THANK YOU, HEAV'NLY FATHER

Luther's Morning Prayer

I thank you, heav'nly Father,
Through Jesus, your dear Son,
That you this night have kept me
From danger and from harm.
Keep me this day from evil,
That all I say and do
Be pleasing and reflective
Of love first shown by you.

I trust my soul and body
Into your loving hands.
All things that I encounter
I leave to your good plans.
Send me your holy angel
To rout the evil one
And crush his meager powers.
Amen, your will be done.

Luther's Evening Prayer

I thank you, heav'nly Father,
Through Jesus, your dear Son,
That graciously you kept me
While daily tasks were done.
I pray that you forgive me
For all my sins and wrongs.
And in your love continue
To keep me all night long.

I trust my soul and body
Into your loving hands.
All things that I encounter
I leave to your good plans.
Send me your holy angel
To rout the evil one
And crush his meager powers.
Amen, your will be done.

Text: Martin Luther
Adapted Katherine Dubke © 2016

Tune: Munich 7676D

CHRISTIANS AND VOCATIONS

The Medieval Church taught that Christians could gain a future reward from God by their own merit. Ordinary lay people could obtain very few merits because they engaged mostly in non-spiritual activities such as raising food or making clothes. Clergy, monks, and nuns, however, gained more merits by reciting the mass, renouncing property, and remaining celibate. The church taught that these merits were collected into a great spiritual treasury that they administered. Often, the church dispensed merits in exchange for favors, goods, or services. Indulgences are one good example: the purchaser received alleged spiritual merits from the treasury in exchange for money.

Luther learned from the Bible that only the merit of Jesus Christ matters. His merit is freely available to every Christian through faith in his sacrificial death and resurrection. This is a free gift, because we are justified by grace alone through faith alone for the sake of Christ alone. Monks do not earn anything before God by living in poverty, celibacy, and obedience. Laity do not lose anything before God by living in marriage, conducting business, or serving in public office. Since all Christians are justified through faith, no role or occupation earns any saving merit at all.

By the same token, our everyday work in ordinary roles and occupations takes on spiritual significance. In thanksgiving, Christians offer their lives as spiritual sacrifices to God by loving their neighbors as they love themselves. Thus, for Christians, being a father or mother is not simply a role to fill. It is a calling from God to serve their children by caring for their physical and spiritual needs. Being a garbage collector or businessperson is not simply a job, but a calling from God to help meet everyone's bodily needs. Being a neighbor is not simply a matter of being friendly, but a calling from God to improve and protect neighbors' possessions, reputations, and lives.

Since the Latin word for "calling" is *vocatio*, Lutherans call these roles "vocations." Each vocation is valuable in God's sight as a way of loving and serving the neighbor. Each comes with its particular challenges and temptations, but also with its particular joys and rewards. And, because salvation comes through faith alone, each is pleasing to God.

TWO KINGDOMS

True story: a boy gets in trouble. When his mother starts to discipline him, the boy responds, "But mom, you should forgive me, because Jesus took my sins away"—to which his mother replies that there are still consequences for his actions. Both mother and child are right, but they are talking about two different things. They are talking about the right-hand and left-hand kingdoms of God.

Luther and his coworkers came to understand that the Triune God works to save us by sending the Holy Spirit to give us faith in Jesus Christ. This work is called God's "right hand kingdom," or "kingdom of grace." Here God uses the means of grace to save sinners. However, the reformers learned from Scripture that God also has a second kind of work. He raises children through parents; he provides for our daily needs through human labor; he preserves the peace through governments. This is called God's "left hand kingdom," or "kingdom of power." Here God uses the law—rewards and punishments, carrots and sticks—to preserve humanity and permit us to enjoy his creation. God is working in both, but his methods and purposes differ.

The reformers saw numerous confusions of these two kingdoms in their day. Many monks thought that their unique, "sacred" work gave them special standing before God, while some German peasants believed that their freedom in Christ should translate into political freedom. The reformers pointed out the errors of both groups. They argued that spiritual authority pursues different ends and uses different means than temporal authority. Our works in the left-hand kingdom do not save us, and our status in the right-hand kingdom is not a blueprint for politics.

Our day has its own confusions of these two kingdoms. Some people believe that they cannot serve God unless their work is "a ministry." Others believe that we can create a Christian nation by enforcing laws consistent with the Scriptures. Others (like the boy above) believe that God's forgiveness should annul just civil punishments. The Reformers point us back to Scripture to learn the truth: God uses temporal rewards and punishments in the left-hand kingdom, but faith can be created only through the means of the right-hand kingdom. Both kingdoms belong to God, but whenever we confuse them, we lose the good news of forgiveness in Christ.

REFORMING EDUCATION FOR ALL

The Reformation forever changed education. In Martin Luther's day, formal education was reserved for boys. Specifically, it was for boys who would go on to be lawyers, doctors, or priests.

The Reformation taught that all Christians are called by God through Christ to love their neighbors. They do this through their many roles in family, community, work, and church (1 Corinthians 7:17, 20; 1 John 4:7-11). This teaching led Luther to see that everyone needs formal education. Everyone needs an education in the liberal arts and sciences so they best understand how to help others through their God-given vocations in life. They also need an education to help them read God's word, receive the Gospel of Jesus Christ in the word, and proclaim that saving word to the world. The temporal and eternal benefits of education equally apply to all— lawyers and businessmen, future fathers and future mothers, politicians and citizens.

Luther was the first person to argue that all boys and girls should receive a formal education and that the state should pay for it. He robustly claimed in support of education:

> A city's best and greatest welfare, safety, and strength consist rather in its having many able, learned, wise, honorable, and well-educated citizens. They can then readily gather, protect, and properly use treasure and all manner of property. (*Luther's Works* 45:356)

This was a watershed moment for education in the West. It is the reason why millions of boys and girls have gone to school in Europe as well as in North, Central, and South America.

The reformation of education still impacts us. As in Luther's day, we too need wise and honorable citizens who thoughtfully and excellently fulfill their callings in family, work, society, and church. We need citizens who identify, analyze, and solve problems in life and do so in ways that promote peace and justice for others. We need citizens who insightfully read God's word and eloquently proclaim its saving message to others. Education is always reforming.

WE ARE BEGGARS

Luther wrote many things during his career.

His final word was a short note in which he wrote briefly about the riches of Holy Scripture. "Let nobody suppose that he has tasted the Holy Scriptures sufficiently unless he has ruled over the churches with the prophets for a hundred years" (AE 54:76). Having himself translated the Bible into German, taught numerous classes, preached many sermons, and written volumes expositing the Word of God, this was his conclusion. He had not tasted the word sufficiently. There were still more riches and blessings to be discovered.

This final humility before the word of God reflects what the Holy Spirit had revealed to him. Everything we receive is a gracious gift of God. The Scriptures are a gracious gift. God's blessings are new to us each day as he richly provides for his children what they can never deserve. And, above all, the new life and salvation that is ours through the death and resurrection of Jesus Christ is a pure gift of grace. "By grace you have been saved through faith. And this is not your own doing; it is the gift of God, not a result of works, so that no one may boast (Ephesians 2:8–9).

Luther reflects all of this in his final sentence on that note. "We are beggars, this is true."

Indeed it is. Thank God it is. We can offer nothing but our sin and brokenness. We are desperate beggars before God in all matters. But God is our gracious Father who provides all our needs from his abundance. Therefore we can joyfully add our assent to Luther's words.

We are beggars. This is true.

ALWAYS REFORMING

Five hundred years ago, an Augustinian monk, reading Scripture, rediscovered Christianity's central teaching. Salvation does not come from human works or efforts but is a free gift of God's grace alone, received by faith alone, in Christ alone. Martin Luther was troubled by practices and teachings in his church that obscured this truth. So he tried to open a dialogue about these issues, posting theses for discussion and debate. Those theses lit a fire that still burns. The core of the Reformation was simply the proclamation of the Gospel for all.

Sinful human nature always tries to supplant the Gospel with our own action. This was the case in the Medieval Church, but the problem did not stop there. Every generation sees similar challenges. Every church faces this temptation. Each Christian is tempted to focus on his or her efforts instead of Christ.

What theses would be posted on the Church's website today? What teachings and practices threaten to obscure the Gospel? What points us away from Jesus?

What theses should be posted in our communities? On your Facebook page? Or on your heart?

Wherever there are sinners, there is always the temptation to obscure the Gospel. And the church is made up of sinners.

God has a remedy. As Luther stated in his first thesis: "When our Lord and Master Jesus Christ said, 'Repent,' he willed the entire life of believers to be one of repentance."

Repent! Turn from this sin and to Christ and his word. In faithful humility, we confess our failures, our self-centeredness, and our pride. We confess our neglect of God's word and our lack of love.

And, like all who come in humble faith, we find that ever-faithful grace and love of God. The church survives her reformations because Christ is her Lord. He calls his church—and each of his children—to renewal. Restoration. Reformation.

> If you abide in my word, you are truly my disciples, and you will know the truth, and the truth will set you free.
>
> –John 8:31b–32

> So if the Son sets you free, you will be free indeed.
>
> –John 8:36

> For by grace you have been saved through faith. And this is not your own doing; it is the gift of God, not a result of works, so that no one may boast. For we

> are his workmanship, created in Christ Jesus for good works, which God prepared beforehand, that we should walk in them.
>
> –Ephesians 2:8–10

Almighty God our heavenly Father, you recall your Church to you and rejoice when sinners repent, grant to your people a steadfast and joyful faith, confidence in your Gospel, and a zeal for witness and service. Through Jesus Christ, your Son, our Lord, who lives and reigns with you and the Holy Spirit, one God, now and forever. Amen.

I AM BROKEN, OH LORD

I am broken, oh Lord.

Shattered into a thousand pieces.

This vessel you perfectly created has failed again.

Not by your design. Vainly I tried to outdo the master. Tried to reshape your work into my own design, thinking I could improve on your beautiful art.

So I am broken.

Frantically seeking to repair the debris. Patching with adulterated clay to hide the damage and feign wholeness. Each concealment highlighting the truth.

I am broken, oh Lord.

Shattered into a thousand pieces.

But you, Lord, are the potter. I am the clay.

Take my dry, brittle fragments, worthless and cast aside, and make them your own.

Plunge them in life-giving water. Drown those worthless shards—and soften them.

There, in your font, make them your clay once more.

As once you formed humanity of dust and earth, take these broken shards and make them your clay.

Shape me anew into your vessel. Whole again. Re-formed into your image.

A fitting vessel once more—but still of clay.

Fill these earthen vessels with your grace, with faith, with Christ.

That re-formed, I might carry you to the world.

Lord, the church you created is broken again.

Shattered into a thousand pieces.

Vainly trying to reshape your perfect art into our own kitschy inferiority.

Made of clay for noble purpose, but broken. Shattered every time when we think we are the potters.

Weakened by fillers and concealments foolishly trying to hide our brokenness. Crushed fragments—but decorated as if to say we are not broken. Not made of dirt.

Pressed and pulled and beaten by selfishness and greed, by hatred and dissension. By trying to conform to the broken patterns of the world.

We ourselves are broken, Lord. Shattered into a thousand pieces. Again.

But you, Lord, are the potter. We are the clay.

Take these brittle shards, worthless and cast aside, and make them your own.

Plunge them in life-giving water. Drown those worthless shards—and soften them.

There, in your water, make them your clay once more. One once more.

Lord, who once formed humanity of dust and earth, take these broken shards and make them your clay.

Spirit who called dry bones to rise into a mighty army,

Savior who, with a word, calls the dead to life,

Take the worthless shards of your church.

Take any -isms and -ologies that do not come from you and drown them in baptismal floods that you might draw them again into your malleable clay.

Re-form us.

That once more, the vessel of your church may rise and your children may be vessels of grace for the world.

You Lord, you alone are the potter, and we are the clay. Reform us again into your image.

Recreate us into your vessel.

Always reform us—into your vessels.

Fit for service.

Glorious because of you.

A HYMN FOR REFORMATION

CHRIST ALONE THE WORLD'S REDEEMER

Christ alone the world's redeemer,
Christ, God's own begotten Son,
Christ, the sacrifice for sinners,
By his death salvation won.
Christ alone our mediator,
Christ alone our great high priest,
In his righteousness, he clothes us.
Christ alone is our true peace.

Word alone, breathed by the Spirit,
Word revealing Christ our Lord,
Living, active voice of Jesus,
Sharper than a two-edged sword.
Word to teach and to admonish,
Word to comfort and to heal.
God's own word endures forever
All his counsel to reveal.

ALWAYS REFORMING

Grace alone, and not our working,
Brings salvation unto all.
Grace alone! Your gifts you give us
As we hear your gentle call.
Unimagined love, exchanging
All our sin for righteousness.
Grace on grace through Christ receiving,
Clothed in his own holiness.

Faith alone, gift of the Spirit,
Can God's gracious gift receive.
Not by human works or effort,
God is calling to believe.
Faith is living, busy, active,
Ever seeking ways to care,
In the least, the lost, the needy,
Seeking Jesus everywhere.

Unto God be praise and glory.
To the Father, and the Son,
And to God the Holy Spirit,
Glory to the Three in One.
Hymned by saints on earth and heaven,
And by angels at his throne.
All creation joins to praise him.
Glory be to God alone!

In Babilone
87 87D

ABOUT CONCORDIA UNIVERSITY IRVINE

The story of Concordia University Irvine dates back to the mid-1950s when a small group of Southern California Lutherans began to plan for a Lutheran college to serve the people of the Pacific Southwest. An extensive search for the "perfect" site led to Irvine, California. In 1976, classes were held for the first time at Christ College Irvine, the original name of the institution. From its humble beginning in a single building with 36 students, Christ College Irvine has become Concordia University Irvine with a student body that continues to expand with each passing year. Today, Concordia University Irvine is a U.S. News Top Tier Regional University that prepares students for their vocations—their various callings in life. CUI offers undergraduate and graduate degree programs in a beautiful Southern California location, with online and regional cohort options. Concordia's undergraduate program is distinctive among universities in California because of its nationally recognized Enduring Questions & Ideas (Q&I) core curriculum, and its Lutheran heritage that provides a thoughtful and caring Christian community that lives out "Grace Alone. Faith Alone." Learn more about us and our programs at www.cui.edu, or call (800) 229-1200.

STEVEN P. MUELLER

The Rev. Dr. Steven P. Mueller serves as Professor of Theology and Dean of Christ College—Concordia University Irvine's school of theology, philosophy, biblical and classical languages, and church vocations.

Made in the USA
Middletown, DE
23 December 2022